Dear
Mr. President

From a Mother

Published by Florida Publishing Group
floridapublishinggroup.com

Book Cover Design: Brianna Lopez

Editor: Monica San Nicolas

Paperback ISBN: 978-1-945812-51-4

Hardback ISBN: 978-1-945812-58-3

DISCLAIMER

This book is designed to provide information on abortion only. This information is provided and sold with the knowledge that the publisher and author do not offer any legal or medical advice. In the case of a need for any such expertise consult with the appropriate professional. This book does not contain all information available on the subject. This book has not been created to be specific to any individual people or organization's situation or needs. Reasonable efforts have been made to make this book as accurate as possible. However, there may be typographical and or content errors. Therefore, this book should serve only as a general guide . This book contains information that might be dated or erroneous and is intended only to educate and entertain. The author and publisher shall have no liability or responsibility to any person or entity regarding any loss or damage incurred, or alleged to have incurred, directly or indirectly, by the information contained in this book or as a result of anyone acting or failing to act upon the information in this book. You hereby agree never to sue and to hold the author and publisher harmless from any and all claims arising out of the information contained in this book. You hereby agree to be bound by this disclaimer, covenant not to sue and release. You may return this book within the guarantee time period for a full refund. All characters appearing in this work are fictitious. Any resemblance to real persons, living or dead, is purely coincidental. The opinions and stories in this book are the views of the author and not that of the publisher.

DEDICATION

"Is human civilization really on the path of progress
or is human society being further degraded with each passing day?"
- Anastasía -

The words of this beautiful woman ignited me.

I dedicate this book to her.
- the author -

Dear Mr. President,

I am a woman who had an abortion
back in the day when it was illegal.
It was performed in a doctor's office,
after hours... discreet and sterile,
found through a friend,
whose older "playboy" brother
had used many times.

I was in high school and in those days
the shame and tainted reputation
were too much to bear.
I simply "had to go through with it."
But as overwhelmingly pressing
as this rationalization was,
this was not what drove me to hysteria.
It was the knowing I am taking a life
that made me break down
that made me barely able to function.
Reacting in the Grip of Fear,
I drove myself forward.

After the "performance,"
the doctor told me to go home.
I would experience severe cramping
and like a heavy period,
to sit on the toilet and
"it" would be discharged.
Any complications, call him and he
would immediately
put me in the hospital.

I went home expecting heavy cramps
and menstrual flow...
To my horror,
my "contractions"
"dumped" a fetus - a baby!
into the toilet.

I vowed
in that instant
never
to have an abortion
again!

Today, women don't have to confront
the truth of what they are doing.
It's all nice and sterile (really covert)
so they don't have to see,
don't have to know.

But a woman knows in her heart,
in her conscience,
in her very soul,
this act is against
the laws of Life,
the laws of Being,
the laws of one's own True Nature,
especially the laws of Woman.
Her True Nature is to Give Life,
not take it.

And what is a Human's true nature?
It is a spiritual nature.
Human is a Spiritual Being.
This is what sets
human beings
apart from all other beings.
What does it mean to be
a Spiritual Being?
It means one can know The Creator.
And can appreciate His Creation.
And this knowing is proof in itself that
there is a Creator.
And it means one can love.
To love is to know God,
for God is Love.
Whenever we love,
God is there, for
God Is Love.

But with our knowing also comes
responsibility,
the responsibility to take care of life,
take care of each other,
to love life,
And to create.

Only Human can create with love.

A sane woman
would never even
contemplate aborting
a child
conceived
in love.

Here we come to the heart
the problem no one is talking about,
the "elephant in the room"
Human's laws are not above God's Laws.
They are inscribed in every
Human's heart.
Some have been written,
not to tell Human what to do,
but to remind those of us who have
lost our way.

Why have so many of us lost our way?
Why do we think we have to be told
by another or a book,
what is good and right,
be told what God says
instead of trusting our own hearts.
Why do we not trust our own inner
knowing, our conscience, our heart?
We go to churches, mosques, temples,
for guidance and support,
and our parents and teachers
pass on the same.
Then why?
It is because <u>no one</u> is teaching about
<u>Human</u> responsibility.

I came from the "free love" generation.
Irresponsibility was conceived in
the generation of free love.
(pun intended)
"Effing" was spun as making love.

"Make love, not war."
But make sure ya got plenty o' birth control.
Over the airwaves, music about love
became music about making love
became music about sex
became chanting about porn.
Now, we have artists who "pornify"
themselves to sell their songs
and call it art.
And all of our X ratings don't mean a thing
when 5-year-olds are trying to gyrate

like ⎯⎯ ⎯⎯. (fill in the blanks)

No one is taught about respect,
self-respect, responsibility.
And the dumbed-down teachers are
teaching dumbed-down children sex,
teaching preteens birth control
and calling it "teaching responsibility."
It's not only dumb, it's oxymoronic.
While the parents of no responsibility
allow a box in their home to
<u>program their children</u>

—as well as themselves—
into accepting that "effing" and horror
and bloody murder is normal, okay,
cool _ _ _ _. (fill in the blanks)

A girl needs to be shown
the beautiful responsibility
she holds in her very Being
to one day help conceive another
Human Being,
cherish it within her as only she can,
nurture it and help it to grow up
with self-respect and self-determinism.

And she needs to be shown
the power entrusted to her
to <u>uphold</u> <u>her</u> <u>responsibility</u>
as a sacred vessel for perpetuating
the Loving Spirit of Creation on Earth.

And that it is
from within her
and through her
that a boy learns love.

A boy needs to be shown that
without a girl (his mother),
he would never have been born.

Sadly, in these times,
many mothers have lost their way.

But if a mother loves her son,
he will love his mother.

And because he loves his mother,
he respects his mother.

And all girls as potential mothers
are, therefore, worthy of respect.

Herein lies his responsibility:
to act honorably.

For <u>without</u> <u>honor</u>,
a boy can never be a true man.

Our children, our youth,
are not being shown their roles as
Human Beings—
the honor, the duty, the responsibility
to care for and about each other and
Life.

As long as all of us are being
overtly and covertly
programmed,
laws will not change us.
It is <u>the programming</u> that
<u>must be changed.</u>

And for those of us who are
too "programmed" to change it:
Go cold turkey.
Turn off the TV.
Start doing that soul-searching.
You have one.
You can find it.
You are one.
You can know yourself.
Listen to your heart.
It's just common sense.
You were born with it.
You know, like, "Hey, this is stupid!"
"Hey, this just ain't right!"
"This is disgusting!"
"This is ugly!"
"This is horrific!"
"This is insane!"
"This is against Human Nature!"
"This is against Creation!"

<u>To be Pro-Life
is not about being
against Pro-Choice!</u>

That is the "Programmer's" spin!

The Choice is really about

Choosing Life, Love, Joy, Beauty,
Creativity, Responsibility
or
Choosing Death, Hate, Grief, Ugly,
Destruction, Care-Less-ness

Generation versus Degeneration
Flourishing versus Decadence
Morality versus Debauchery

This is the weakness of the
<u>Pro-Choice Law</u>:
It <u>legitimizes</u>
<u>degeneration</u>
<u>decadence</u>
<u>debauchery</u>.

Make the laws of the state be
the laws of the Human Spirit

as was intended in our Constitution.

Make Pro-Life be

the Law of waking people up
to the depths we have succumbed to,
and the opportunity to find ourselves
and to ethically, morally, and spiritually
empower ourselves.

We're all on this ship together.
We have all succumbed to depravity
to a degree.
But, being Human,
we can save ourselves.
We can learn from our mistakes.
We can change, as you yourself have.

Make the farm-out-fetus clinics
illegal,
but allow doctors (such as I had)
to sever the umbilical cord of the
fetus
in their office and send the mother
home,
so she can see the unborn child she
helped murder be flushed down the
toilet.
May the doctor awaken,
to the hell he makes.
And may the mother's horror,
awaken her
to make a difference
in a world that has lost its purpose.

And may this letter open her eyes
open her mind
open her heart
to make this choice
before she goes to the doctor
And open her lover's heart/mind
to respect himself
and so respect her

And may this letter open the eyes
of the many who think they are free,
when they are really just
carnally programmed copycats,
unable to think for themselves,
unable to act willfully.

You are the head of the spear of
the force that is rising up from hell.
The awake, the righteous,
the indignant, the honorable,
the good - are a wave.
We will buoy you up.

Message to my fellow Human Beings:

Witness: The Destroyer
in the maker or makings of all that is
artificial and evil.

Evil spelled backwards is Live.
Evil has long been running this world.
Its banner of intent is Death:

Death to Our Good
Death to Our Truth
Death to Our Beauty
Death to Our Joy
Death to Our Courage
Death to Our Creativity
Death to Our Self-Determinism
Death to Our Will
Death to Our Love
Death to Our Mind
Death to The Human Spirit

Because God is The Creator
God Ultimately Wins
God enters in when we allow

Allow

Good to come Alive

Truth to come Alive

Beauty to come Alive

Joy to come Alive

Courage to come Alive

Creativity to come Alive

Self-Determinism to come Alive

Will to come Alive

Love to come Alive

Mind to come Alive

Your God Given Human Spirit to Come

Alive

Wake Up to Who You Really Are!

Witness: Our Creator
through our
HeartMind

How could we witness if not for God,
Who has endowed HuMan with Spirit.
<u>It is the Soul that witnesses!</u>

It is not artificial – It is Real!

It is not dead – It is Alive! Eternally!

It is not uncreating – It is Creative!

It was not, is not, and never can be

made by an alien or in a laboratory.

A mere physical entity

can never create a Soul.

Only The Soul can bear witness

to all these things

And it is That which ultimately chooses!

I ask all Souls who read or hear this,

"Which do you choose?"

With love and support,
A Mother